Masterpieces: Artists and Their Works

Mary Cassatt

by Blake A. Hoena

W
FRANKLIN WATTS
LONDON•SYDNEY

This edition first published in 2004 by

Franklin Watts
96 Leonard Street
London
EC2A 4XD

Franklin Watts Australia
45-51 Huntley Street
Alexandria
NSW 2015

ISBN: 0 7496 5424 4

Printed in Hong Kong

Consultant: Joan Lingen, Ph.D. Professor of Art History, Clarke College, Iowa, USA

Cover Art: *Breakfast in Bed* by Mary Cassat.

Editorial Credits
Heather Kindseth, series designer; Juliette Peters, book designer; Alta Schaffer, photo researcher; Karen Risch, product planning editor

Photo Credits
Archives of American Art, Smithsonian Institution/Mary Cassatt, after 1900. Research material on Mary Cassatt and James A. MacNeill Whistler 1872–1975, cover (right)
Bridgeman Art Library/Los Angeles County Museum of Art, 4; Mellon Coll., National Gallery of Art, Washington, D.C., USA, 12
Chester Dale Collection, Image 2002 Board of Trustees, National Gallery of Art, Washington, D.C., 20
Chicago Historical Society, 18
Corbis/Philadelphia Museum of Art, 6, 16
Montclair Art Museum, Montclair, N.J., Gift of the Max Kade Foundation, 1958.1, 8
SuperStock/The Huntington Library, Art Collections, and Botanical Gardens, San Marino, CA, cover (left)
The Roland P. Murdock Collection, Wichita Art Museum, Wichita, Kansas, 14
Sterling and Francine Clark Art Institute, Williamstown, Massachusetts, 10

Table of Contents

Mary Cassatt 5
Young Mary 7
Paris 9
Mary's Travels 11
Edgar Degas 13
Mothers and Children 15
Prints 17
Modern Woman 19
Mary's Fame 21

Timeline 22
Useful Websites 23
Glossary 24
Index 24

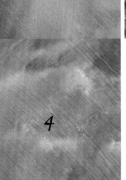

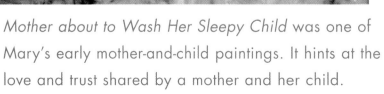

Mother about to Wash Her Sleepy Child was one of Mary's early mother-and-child paintings. It hints at the love and trust shared by a mother and her child.

Mary Cassatt

Mary Cassatt (1844–1926) lived during a time when women were not encouraged to be artists. Most people felt that women should stay at home and raise a family. They did not think women could earn money as artists.

Also, Mary was an American. In the 1800s, art critics did not respect American artists. They didn't think that Americans knew about **culture** and art.

Mary did not let people's ideas about women and Americans stop her. She studied art and worked hard. She was the only American invited to join a group of artists called the **Impressionists**. Mary's talent and hard work earned respect for women and American artists.

Mary created many well-known pieces of art. She is best known for her paintings of family scenes. She especially enjoyed painting mothers with their children, as in *Breakfast in Bed* (shown on the cover).

In *Alexander and His Son*, Mary's brother Alexander sits with his son Robert. Mary shows the closeness between father and son by giving them similar expressions.

Young Mary

Mary was born in Allegheny City, in Pennsylvania USA, on 22nd May 1844. This town is now a part of the city of Pittsburgh. Her parents were Robert and Katherine Cassatt. Mary had three brothers and one sister.

When Mary was seven, her family moved to Europe. Her parents wanted to show their children European culture. The children learned foreign languages and visited galleries and museums. Mary developed a love for art while in Europe. The Cassatts moved back to the United States in 1855.

At the age of 16, Mary went to the Pennsylvania Academy of Fine Arts. She studied drawing and painting. She also learned about **anatomy**, the study of the human body. Artists study this to learn how to make realistic pictures and statues of people.

When Mary was 21, she moved to Paris to study art. Many famous artists lived in Paris at the time. Paris also had better art schools and museums than the United States did.

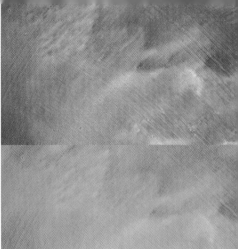

The Salon's judges originally rejected *The Young Bride.*
They chose to display it after Mary darkened its background.

8

Paris

At first, Mary had a bad time in Paris. Teachers at many art schools did not want to teach women. The main art school, Ecole des Beaux-Arts, did not accept women as students.

Mary found other ways to study. She took private painting lessons from art teachers. She also spent a great deal of time at the Louvre Museum in Paris. There, she copied well-known paintings. Artists often learn how to paint by copying the work of famous artists.

In 1868, at the age of 24, Mary's hard work was rewarded. The Salon displayed her painting *The Mandolin Player*. The Salon was a popular art gallery in Paris. People from around the world came to see and buy art there.

Years later, Mary displayed *Ida* and *The Young Bride* at the Salon. These paintings helped her to gain respect as an artist and people began to buy her paintings.

In *The Young Woman Offering the Panal to the Toreador*, the people look as if they could be talking. Mary tried to show the relationships between people in her art.

Mary's Travels

During the early 1870s, Mary travelled. She went to the cities of Pittsburgh and Chicago to try to sell her work. The Great Fire of 1871 broke out while Mary was there. The fire destroyed a large part of downtown Chicago and many of Mary's early paintings were burned.

In late 1871, Mary returned to Europe to study. She copied old paintings in Italy. She looked at famous works of art in the Netherlands, Belgium and Spain.

In Spain, Mary spent several months in the town of Seville. There, she studied Spanish art and painted the people she saw.

While in Seville, Mary's work began to change. Many of her earlier paintings were portraits that used dark colours. Her Seville paintings were more colourful. They showed the bright costumes of the Spanish people. Mary also began to paint scenes from everyday life while in Seville. These paintings showed the relationships between people.

Little Girl in a Blue Armchair was Mary's first attempt at **Impressionism**. This painting captures a moment of everyday life by showing a girl sitting in a natural, relaxed way.

Edgar Degas

Mary grew tired of painting in the style that the Salon's judges liked. They wanted to display traditional paintings. These paintings often had dark backgrounds and were very lifelike.

In 1877, Mary met Edgar Degas. Degas belonged to the Impressionists. Members of this art movement included well known artists Claude Monet and Auguste Renoir.

Impressionists worked with bright colours and did not worry about painting lifelike pictures. They tried to show how a scene looked at a quick glance. Impressionists used broken brush strokes of one solid colour. They did not blend colours together as they painted. This style made their work look splotchy up close. However, from a distance, the picture in a painting could easily be seen.

Degas invited Mary to join the Impressionists. In 1879, she displayed 11 paintings at an Impressionist art exhibition in Paris.

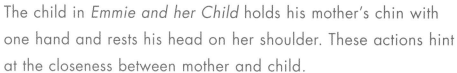

The child in *Emmie and her Child* holds his mother's chin with one hand and rests his head on her shoulder. These actions hint at the closeness between mother and child.

Mothers and Children

Mary's paintings were different to other Impressionists. Most Impressionists painted outdoor scenes but Mary liked to paint indoor scenes of people. She wanted to show the relationships between people in her art. Many of her paintings are **portraits** of her family and friends.

Mary painted people doing everyday activities. She painted people drinking tea, reading the newspaper, going to the theatre, and sewing. Her paintings made everyday events seem important.

One of Mary's favourite subjects was mothers with their children. Mary never married or had children of her own. But in her art, she was able to show the love that mothers and children share.

Mary's art helped show the importance of women in society. By painting women reading, she hinted at their intelligence. By painting mothers, she showed that women are important as carers.

In Mary's print *The Letter,* the woman is deep in thought. Mary liked to show women performing everyday activities, such as thinking about a letter.

Prints

In 1879, Mary began to create etchings. **Etchings** are pictures created on a metal plate. Artists cover the plate with ink to make prints of the picture. Etchings allow artists to make many copies of the same picture.

Prints are less expensive to make than paintings. Prints are also cheaper for people to buy. Many artists create etchings so more people can enjoy their work.

Mary joined the **Society** of Painters-Engravers in the late 1880s. This group of artists made prints. In 1889 and 1890, Mary showed her prints at the Painter-Engravers exhibitions in Paris. But in 1891, she was not allowed to display her work because she was not French.

Mary decided to have her own exhibition. She displayed 10 prints and some of her paintings at an art gallery in Paris. Many of her prints showed women doing simple things, like bathing or dressing. People were amazed by how colourful Mary's prints were.

In the centre of *Modern Woman*, a woman hands an apple to a young girl. Mary wanted this scene to show that the hard work of modern women made it easier for young girls to gain knowledge.

Modern Woman

Mary was asked to paint a **mural** for the 1893 World's Columbian Exposition. This fair in Chicago celebrated advances in business, science, and art.

Mary's painting was shown in the Woman's Building. This building held displays about important women **activists** and scientists. It also presented examples of women's arts and crafts from around the world.

Mary called her painting *Modern Woman*. Its centre section showed women gathering fruit from the Tree of Knowledge and Science. The right section showed women dancing and playing music. The left section showed three women chasing after an angel-like figure. This scene represented women seeking fame. Mary's painting honoured the work of modern women.

After the fair, *Modern Woman* was removed from the Woman's Building. No one knows what happened to the painting after that but it was lost and probably destroyed. Only pictures of the painting remain.

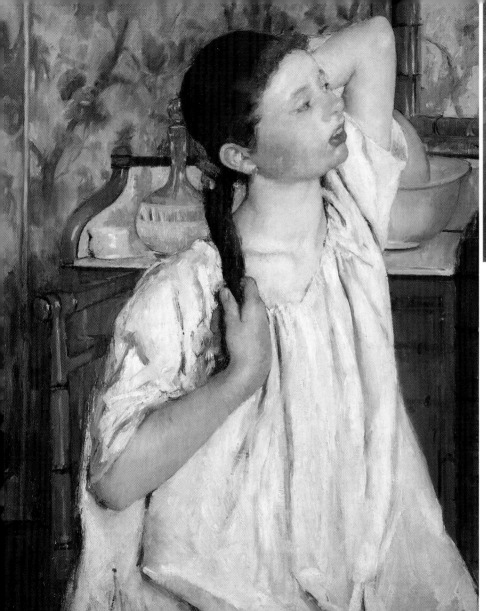
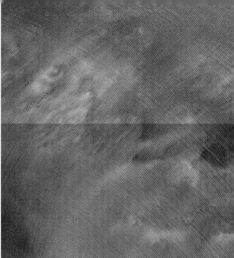

Edgar Degas bought *Girl Arranging Her Hair* from Mary. After his death, many people thought Degas had painted it. They did not think a woman could create such a skillful work of art.

Mary's Fame

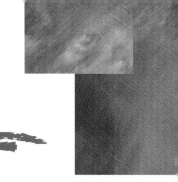

In the early 1900s, Mary began to lose her sight. She could not see well enough to work during the last years of her life. On 14th June 1926, Mary died. She was 82.

Mary achieved a great deal as an artist. Her work gained recognition for American artists in Europe. She also introduced Americans to European styles of art.

In her art, Mary showed the importance of women. Through her success she also made people realise that women could be great artists.

Today, people can see Mary's art in museums. The Philadelphia Museum of Art in Pennsylvania and the Metropolitan Museum of Art in New York display many of her paintings and prints.

Timeline

1844 - Mary Cassatt is born in Pennsylvania, USA on 22nd May.

1851 - Mary's family moves to Europe.

1860 - Mary begins her studies at the Pennsylvania Academy of Fine Arts.

1861 - The U.S. Civil War begins; the war ends in 1865.

1866 - Mary moves to Paris, France, to study art.

1868 - The Salon displays *The Mandolin Player*.

1871 - The Great Fire of 1871 destroys much of downtown Chicago; many of Mary's early paintings are destroyed in the fire.

1877 - The artist Edgar Degas introduces Mary to the Impressionists.

1879 - Mary exhibits her paintings with the Impressionists.

1880 - Mary paints *Mother about to Wash Her Sleepy Child*.

1886 - Mary paints *Girl Arranging Her Hair.*

1891 - Mary shows her prints and paintings in a solo exhibit.

1893 - *Modern Woman* is displayed in the Woman's Building at the World's Columbian Exposition in Chicago.

1914 - The First World War begins; the war ends in 1918.

1926 - Mary dies on 14th June.

Useful Websites

www.ibiblio.org/wm/paint/auth/cassatt/
This site offers biographical detail as well as lots of fascinating information about the paintings themselves.

www.nga.gov/collection/gallery/cassatt/cassatt.html
This is the official site for The National Gallery of Art in the US. It is very thorough if a little bit overwhelming and provides lots of information. Each page is a different room in the gallery and you can join the online tour.

www.artencyclopedia.com/artists/cassatt_mary.html
This is a comprehensive site that showcases practically all of Cassatt's paintings whilst listing exhibitions and providing links and reading lists.

www.abcgallery.com/C/cassat/cassatt.html
This site includes lots of biographical information and useful links and images to download.

Note to parents and teachers
Every effort has been made by the Publishers to ensure that these websites are suitable for children; that they are of the highest educational value, and that they contain no inappropriate or offensive material. However, because of the nature of the Internet, it is impossible to guarantee that the contents of these sites will not be altered. We strongly advise that Internet access is supervised by a responsible adult.

GLOSSARY

activist — a person who supports an important cause; during the late 1800s and early 1900s, many women activists fought for the right for women to vote.

anatomy — the study of the human body

critic — someone who reviews art, books, or movies

culture — the way of life, ideas, customs, and traditions for a group of people

etching — a picture created on a metal plate; an artist uses an etching to make prints of a picture.

Impressionism — an art style in which artists painted in broken brush strokes

mural — a large work of art on a wall or a ceiling

portrait — a drawing or painting of a person

society — a large group of people who have similar interests, activities, and traditions

Index

Americans 5, 7, 17, 21
body, the 7
Chicago 11, 19
Degas, Edgar 13, 20
family 5, 6, 7, 15
Impressionism 5, 12, 13, 15

mothers 4, 5, 14, 15
Paris 7, 9, 13, 17
Salon 8, 9, 13
Seville 11
studies 5, 7, 9, 11
women 5, 9, 15, 19, 21